Once upon a time there was a little girl named Kaya Rain. When her daddy would tell her that Grandpa was coming to visit she would sit at the window and wait and wait and wait.

W hen Grandpa finally gets to Kaya's house, he and Kaya play games all night.

They would play Match.

They would
color.

They would dance.

And the one thing that Kaya Rain was most good at was putting puzzles together.

Then later at night her Daddy would say,

"Time for bed!"

And Kaya Rain would say,

"Pretty soon!"

So Grandpa mentioned that they have to get up early for pancakes, and Kaya Rain would run up the stairs,

jump into her bed, and wait quietly for her daddy to come and tuck her in, and kiss her goodnight.

Early the next morning Grandpa would
hear little feet get out of bed and come
down the stairs as quiet as a mouse, and

snuggle up to him. "Good morning", Grandpa said gently, but Kaya Rain said nothing, only looking at Grandpa with joy. "What is it you want?" askes Grandpa. "Pancakes?", she answers with a smile.

In the spring she and Grandpa would walk, and on their way Kaya Rain would splash in the mud puddles.

She would look in the wall for spiders in their homes.

In the summer they would walk, and on their way Kaya Rain would smell all the new flowers.

"Yum, they smell good!"

She would see a bee busy at his work.

In the fall they would walk, and on their way

Kaya Rain would play in the fallen leaves.

She would splash in the puddles,

and she would pick pine cones for Grandpa to carry.

In the winter they would walk and on their way Kaya Rain would blaze the trail through the deep snow.

"Excuse me snow, excuse me!"

she would whisper.

She would stop to see the spiders.

"Where did they go, Grandpa?"

She would look for all the sweet smelling flowers.

Then finally at the end of their walks

they would make it to the Pancake Café.

There Kaya Rain and Grandpa would share a big stack of pancakes with strawberries, blueberries, bananas and the biggest swirl of whipping cream on the top.

"Just like coffee, Grandpa!"

Grandpa would have his coffee and drop an ice cube in it, and Kaya Rain would have her chocolate milk and drop an ice cube in it.

Then after their big breakfast they would start back home. "Carry, Grandpa Pancakes?" she asked softly.

So Grandpa Pancakes lifts her all covered with snow onto his shoulders,

and Kaya Rain would fall

fast

asleep.

The End.

Made in the USA
Charleston, SC
21 May 2014